Frank Lloyd Wright's Fallingwater

Frank Lloyd Wright's Fallingwater

Photographs by Ezra Stoller

Introduction by Neil Levine

Princeton Architectural Press • New York

The BUILDING BLOCKS series presents the masterworks of modern architecture through the iconic images of acclaimed architectural photographer Ezra Stoller.

ADDITIONAL TITLES IN THE SERIES

The Chapel at Ronchamp
The Salk Institute
The Seagram Building
Taliesin West
The TWA Terminal
The United Nations
The Yale Art + Architecture Building

Contents

Introduction	1
Plates	15
Drawings & Plans	83
Key to Images	89

Frank Lloyd Wright photographed by Ezra Stoller in 1945 at the First Unitarian Meeting House (1949–51), Madison, Wisconsin.

Introduction

Neil Levine

FALLINGWATER IS SURELY the most photogenic private house built in the twentieth century, and probably the most photographed. Despite its remote location in the foothills of southwestern Pennsylvania's Appalachian Mountains, over 130,000 camera-wielding tourists visit it every year. Fallingwater's protean image can be found on everything from T-shirts and tote bags to calendars and coffee mugs in bookstores and gift shops around the country and throughout the world.

The photographic reproduction of the Kaufmann family's weekend retreat began even before the house was completely finished and occupied. In the late fall of 1937, Bill Hedrich shot the building for a special issue of *Architectural Forum* devoted to the recent work of its architect, Frank Lloyd Wright. The results, along with other photographs taken by John McAndrew and Luke Swank, formed the basis of a one-building exhibition at New York's Museum of Modern Art, organized by McAndrew, the museum's Curator of Architecture and Industrial Art, and held in early 1938. The Hedrich photographs, particularly one taken from below the first falls, which was used for the cover of the exhibition catalog and as a gatefold in *Forum*, became iconic, establishing the building's image for nearly a third of a century.[1]

It was only when the house became public (Edgar Kaufmann, Jr. ceded it to the Western Pennsylvania Conservancy in 1963) that other professional photographers were given the chance to revise how the building would be seen and understood. Ezra Stoller was the first, having been commissioned by Arthur Drexler, then director of MOMA's Department of Architecture and Design, to do a series of large color transparencies for an exhibition in November 1963 celebrating the opening of the house to the public. Among those who followed him have been Yukio Futagawa, Harold Corsini, Thomas Heinz, Christopher Little, Paul Rocheleau, and Robert Ruschak. It was difficult for many, especially at the beginning, to avoid certain angles and points of view that Hedrich had established as "right." It was easier, on the other hand, to define the character and meaning of the interior space, since it had hardly been furnished when Hedrich took his few, relatively unimpressive photographs of it in 1937. And it was also easier to portray a sense of the rich and complex interaction between building and landscape than was possible in the bleak, nearly winter conditions in which Hedrich worked. But that could also be a trap: our impressions of Fallingwater, more than almost any other building, depend on the seasons and change with them.

Sometimes a photographer has the luxury of choosing precisely when to shoot a subject. Other times the commission will be determined by a date of publication or, as in the case of Stoller's trip to Fallingwater in 1963, an upcoming exhibition. Although Drexler felt that Stoller's transparencies, taken in the early fall, displayed an "elegiac, luminous delicacy," Stoller himself was "dissatisfied" with the overly "obscuring and gaudy fall foliage" and the fact that there was "not enough water in the stream." Having tried, to no avail, to convince those responsible to allow him to redo the work to his satisfaction, he eventually returned on his own, eight years later, feeling it was his "duty...to architecture and to Wright."[2] Stoller had by then worked with most of the major architects of the period, including Mies van der Rohe and Le Corbusier, and had photographed some of their most significant buildings. But "Wright was the only...real genius that I ever met," he later said, and "Fallingwater is pretty much his *magnum opus.*"[3] Looking at the photographs from Stoller's two campaigns side by side in this beautifully produced book, we are invited to contemplate not only how a building may be seen to change in time but also how the process of photographic representation can be used to clarify and bring into focus an understanding of that building's underlying idea.

One could endlessly debate whether Fallingwater is Wright's "*magnum opus*" if the discussion is limited to Wright's work alone—other obvious candidates are Taliesin, the Guggenheim Museum, Taliesin West, and Unity Temple. But there would certainly be less argument if one expanded the field to modern architecture as a whole. While most of Wright's work is seen as outside the modernist mainstream— either prior or eccentric to it—Fallingwater takes its place firmly within it while at the same time epitomizing the "organic" philosophy of design Wright maintained as his alone. Coming after a period of several decades in which he had done little building of renown in this country, and following shortly on the heels of the International Style exhibition at the Museum of Modern Art in which he was featured as a superannuated progenitor, Fallingwater was very much intended by Wright to challenge any such view and to prove that he could meet the younger European architects on their own terms. It did precisely that (witness the exhibition devoted to it at MOMA in

3

1938) and continues to define the point at which Wright and orthodox modernism most prominently intersect.

The commission came at a most opportune moment from a most willing and receptive client. After going virtually bankrupt in the late 1920s and almost losing his own house and studio in Wisconsin, Wright founded the apprenticeship-based Taliesin Fellowship in 1932 as a first step toward reorganizing his practice. A small house in Minneapolis for Nancy and Malcolm Willey came into the office that same year (built 1933–34), but it was only with Fallingwater, the second of the Fellowship's commissions to be constructed, that Wright's "second career" took off. The client, Edgar Kaufmann, was the owner of the largest department store in Pittsburgh and a leading citizen of that city. Interested and active in civic affairs, he began corresponding with Wright in the late summer of 1934 about ways of improving Pittsburgh's urban infrastructure. After his son, Edgar, Jr., joined the Fellowship in October, Kaufmann and his wife, Liliane, visited Taliesin the following month and clearly fell under its "charm."[4] A short time later he invited Wright to Pittsburgh, ostensibly to discuss various civic projects; but when Wright came in December he was not only asked to redesign Kaufmann's department store office but also to produce a design for a weekend house for the family on their 1600-acre estate in a rugged upland forest area of the Allegheny plateau, two hours south of Pittsburgh, between the towns of Ohiopyle and Mill Run.

Kaufmann took Wright to visit the rural site just before Christmas. The architect was apparently most impressed with the area around Bear Run, where the rushing mountain stream drops in a series of dramatic falls over stone ledges and large boulders strewn in its bed, and where Kaufmann told him the family liked to swim, picnic, and sunbathe. What defined the site for Wright, and what would ultimately determine his design, was the pervasive sound and rhythm

4

Taliesin, Hillside, Wisconsin, begun 1911. View looking northwest in 1945. Wright thought of Taliesin as a lure: prospective clients were invited to the compound to experience his architecture as a complete way of life.

Taliesin. View of the drafting room in 1945.

of the whitewater. He wrote to Kaufmann on his return to Wisconsin that "the visit to the waterfall in the woods stays with me and a domicile has taken vague shape in my mind to the music of the stream."[5] Little did Kaufmann realize that Wright was contemplating building the house *over* the falls rather than on the opposite bank, looking at them. Wright's desire was to involve all the senses in the appreciation of the site, not just the visual one. Cantilevering the house over the falls as an "extension of the cliff" allowed him to incorporate the moving water within a multilayered space that was designed, as he said, for "one who liked to listen to the waterfall" and thus be constantly reminded of it.[6] The name Fallingwater, which Wright gave to the house, was meant to describe the programmatic identity and dynamic relationship between building and site.

The actual design of Fallingwater was worked out by the following fall. In March 1935, Wright received a topographical map of the specific area chosen, and visited the site for a second time in the early summer before presenting the project to Kaufmann at Taliesin in September. He visited the site a third time, in October, just after sending a set of plans to Kaufmann. The first set of working drawings was produced in January 1936, by which time the quarrying of stone, about 500 feet downstream from the house, had already begun. Construction proceeded throughout 1936 and 1937 (the guest house farther uphill was completed two years later, in 1939). Wright made at least two more trips to the site during construction, partly to deal with engineering issues that arose when Kaufmann asked for outside opinions, most of which confirmed his worst fears regarding the adequacy of Wright's specifications for reinforcing the concrete cantilevers. The Pittsburgh engineering firm of Metzger-Richardson, hired by Kaufmann, redrew Wright's plans to double the number of steel rods in the concrete beams of the first-floor living room and the second-floor master bedroom supported by it. Wright was outraged, but could do little about it. As soon as the formwork was removed, both floor slabs deflected more than they should have, which Wright blamed on the contractor's failure to camber them. And despite the additional steel, the cantilevered terraces have continued to deflect to the extent that the Western Pennsylvania Conservancy was recently forced to undertake a major repair program to stabilize the living room floor.

Fallingwater has suffered from an extraordinarily minimalist attitude toward detailing on Wright's part that affected everything from the reinforcing of the main structural members to the provision of adequate flashing at doors and windows. In some cases this can be understood in terms of a desire to have interior and exterior space appear to be continuous and completely uninterrupted by any obvious mechanical intervention. But in others, as with the skimpy application of reinforcing rods, one can only deduce that this was a building where Wright was not only pushing the envelope but also relishing the risk-taking involved. Fallingwater is a study in contrasts where extreme opposites are held in precarious balance and called upon to produce totally unexpected effects. Vertical walls and piers of roughly laid stone support horizontal terraces and slabs of concrete that appear to slice through them. The thick, rounded parapets of the two main terraces emphasize the plastic weight of the concrete. Visually, this weight is negated by the light, apricot-colored paint with which the terraces are coated, an effect that would have been even more palpable had Wright been allowed to surface them in gold leaf as he originally intended. Seen head-on, from the road on the opposite bank, these parapets look like flat floating bands, distended in space. But from the lower bank of the stream, they echo the shape and disposition of the two stone ledges that create the falls beneath them while at the same time reflecting the movement of the cascading whitewater. Inside the house, the living room floor, which hovers in space above the stream, is laden with heavy waxed flagstones that catch the light in such a way as to look like water rippling over the stream bed itself. Finally, as if to annul its very function, the floor is disrupted in front of the fireplace, where an existing boulder protrudes through it, and again, in the opposite corner of the room, where a glass-enclosed hatch opens to allow the sound and moisture of the stream to penetrate the room—and to allow the inhabitant, by means of a suspended stairway, to descend from the metaphoric to the literal and thus experience their interaction at Fallingwater in a truly kinesthetic way.

Given its complexity, Fallingwater can be read and interpreted—in words or photographic images—in many different ways. Focusing on its daring cantilevering makes it a powerful expression of modernist gravity-defying form. Seeing it in terms of the intersecting orthogonals and overlapping planes of its De Stijl-like geometry puts one in mind of its historical relation to the International Style polemic. Emphasizing its role as a retreat in nature allows one to link it to a long tradition of villa architecture and picturesque design. Taking into account Wright's own description of it as "an extension of the cliff" shaped to "the music of the stream," Fallingwater, as his name for it implies, becomes an abstraction of the natural environment represented in architectural terms, a phenomenon having a temporal as well as a spatial dimension.

Stoller's photographs explore all these possibilities, although, in the end, a very distinctive impression of the place emerges. Some of the views from below the falls describe the metaphoric role the forms play in the landscape while others, especially those closer up, highlight the dramatic cantilevering. Of the former, a shot taken from below the second falls, where the main terraces are approximately parallel to what would be the horizon line, is one of the first photographs of the house

Wright at the First Unitarian Meeting House in 1945.

that captures a sense of its embeddedness in the landscape and of its reciprocal relationship to it [PAGE 17]. This was a product of Stoller's return trip in 1971. Indeed, one can feel the frustration Stoller apparently felt on his first trip, when there was not enough water in the stream to make the terraces and parapets in the closer-up views resonate with the falls and seem less literally concrete. Many of his later images reveal much more fully the dialectic of abstraction and representation that creates the tension in Fallingwater's forms, but paradoxically it is the photographs from 1963 that seem to express with greater poetry Stoller's own response to the place. It is a complicated vision of an architecture hardly disentangled from nature, yet resplendently declarative. By contrast, and almost as if in relief, the interiors from this same first campaign are calming, encompassing, and serenely seen, the first interior views of a Fallingwater lived in and furnished. Although later photographers would have the advantage of a more carefully selected and pruned interior decoration (the removal of the scatter rugs in the living room being a most obvious example), none would give a better sense of the light, the texture, the materiality, and the transparency of these spaces defined by stone and water yet seemingly aloft in a forest of trees.

It is often said, and Stoller seems to have agreed, that photographs can never fully represent a building. While this is no doubt true, they can and usually do come fairly close. But Fallingwater is unique in ways that will always prevent it from being more than marginally understood without its being physically present to the subject. First there is the sound of the water, not to speak of its atmospheric effects. The senses of touch, smell, and sound are always an integral aspect of the experience of the house and its setting. But perhaps even more important, though more elusive, is the factor of time. The moving stream and waterfalls are a part of the house that can never be stopped. It is a simple but profound fact. No other building depends as completely and as undeniably on the passage of time as Fallingwater. Never is this more apparent than at dusk, when the last tour ends and one is asked to leave the grounds. It may seem silly, but the natural reaction is to assume that as the lights are turned off in the house the falls will be shut off with them. And when that does not happen, one begins to grasp the complex and irreducible reality of Fallingwater.

NOTES

1. See "Frank Lloyd Wright," *Architectural Forum* 68 (January 1938): 36–47; and John McAndrew, *A New House by Frank Lloyd Wright on Bear Run, Pennsylvania* (New York: Museum of Modern Art, January 1938). The best history of the house is Donald Hoffmann, *Fallingwater: The House and Its History*, 2d rev. ed. (New York: Dover, 1993). Edgar Kaufmann, Jr. published his memories and thoughts in *Fallingwater: A Frank Lloyd Wright Country House* (New York: Abbeville Press, 1986). An extended analysis of the house appears in my book, *The Architecture of Frank Lloyd Wright* (Princeton: Princeton University Press, 1996), 216–53.

2. *Ezra Stoller: Photographs of Architecture, 1939–1980*, introduction by Arthur Drexler (New York: Max Protetch Gallery, 1980), n.p.; and William S. Saunders, *Modern Architecture: Photographs by Ezra Stoller* (New York: Harry N. Abrams, 1990), 76.

3. George Goodwin, unpublished audio interview of Ezra Stoller, 22 September 1993, 26, 23.

4. Just a few years before the Kaufmann visit, he wrote to his friend and former client Darwin D. Martin, saying that "Taliesin works like a charm on everybody that comes within its atmosphere." Frank Lloyd Wright-Darwin D. Martin Papers, University Archives, State University of New York, Buffalo, 7 September 1929, Box 5-25, MS 22.8.

5. Bruce Brooks Pfeiffer, ed., *Frank Lloyd Wright: Letters to Clients* (Fresno: Press at California State University, 1986), 82.

6. "Frank Lloyd Wright," *Architectural Forum*, 36.

Plates

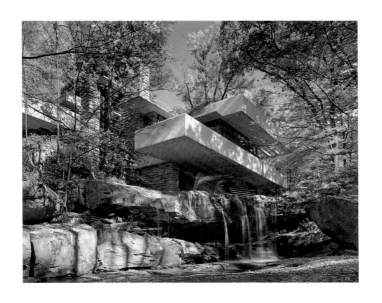

35

Drawings & Plans

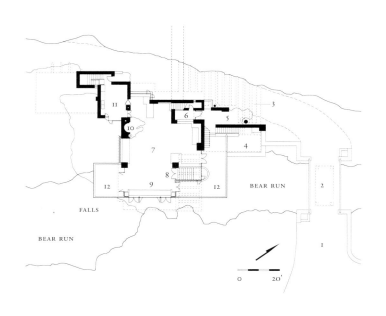

11

10

6 5 3

7

4

8

12 9 12 BEAR RUN 2

FALLS

BEAR RUN 1

0 20'

Plan of ground floor

1. ENTRY DRIVE   5. LOGGIA   9. WINDOW SEAT

2. BRIDGE   6. ENTRY   10. HEARTH

3. TRELLIS   7. LIVING ROOM   11. KITCHEN

4. PLUNGE   8. HATCH   12. TERRACE

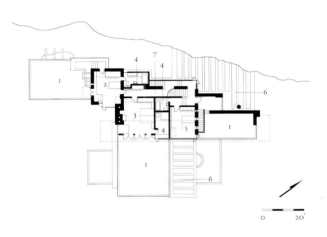

Plan of second floor

1. TERRACE

2. DRESSING ROOM-
   STUDY

3. MASTER BEDROOM

4. BATHROOM

5. GUEST ROOM

6. TRELLIS

7. HALL

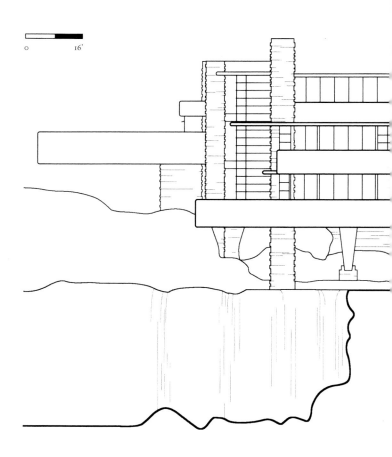

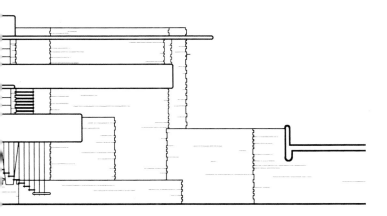

Elevation from opposite bank of Bear Run

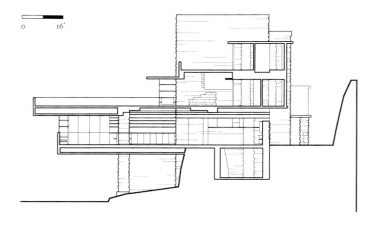

Section along northwest/southeast axis

Key to Photographs

FRONTISPIECE: View from the stream bed (1971)*

17   View from below second falls (1971)
18–9   View from stream bed below second falls (1971)
20   View from below first falls (1963)
21   View from below first falls (1971)
22   View from stream bed below first falls (1963)
23   View from stream bed below first falls (1963)
24   View from stream bed below second falls (1963)
25   View from directly below first falls (1963)
26–7   View of cantilevers from falls (1963)
28–9   Facade from the southeast (1963)
30–1   Facade from the southeast (1963)
32–3   View of facade looking west (1963)
34   View from entry drive (1963)
35   View from east with bridge (1963)
36   View of bridge from stream bed (1963)
37   View of bridge from stream bed (1963)
38   View west from bridge (1963)
39   View west from bridge (1971)
40–1   Facade from bridge (1963)
42   View northwest from stream bed (1963)
43   View southwest from entry drive (1963)
44–5   View of hatch from stream bed (1963)
46   View southwest from entry drive (1963)
47   View southwest from entry drive (1971)

48–9   View southwest from woods (1971)
50   View southwest from driveway (1971)
51   View of trellis and driveway (1963)
52   View east of upper terrace (1963)
53   View east of upper terrace (1971)
54–5   View of upper terrace (1963)
57   Entry seen from loggia (1963)
58   Entry seen from living room (1963)
59   Living room seen from entry (1963)
60–1   View of living room looking east (1963)
62   Living room sitting area (1963)
63   Hatch to stream bed (1963)
64–5   Hearth area looking south (1963)
66–7   Hearth area looking west (1963)
68–9   Sitting area (1963)
70   Living room looking north (1963)
71   Dining area (1963)
72   Kitchen (1963)
73   Stairs to upper level (1963)
74   Stairs with view to dining area (1963)
75   Stairwell with view to dressing room-study (1963)
76   Master bedroom (1963)
77   Guest bedroom with desk (1963)
78   View from terrace looking west (1963)
79   View from terrace looking north (1963)
80–1   View through trees along driveway (1971)

*Dates indicate the year photograph was taken. All photographs by Ezra Stoller.

Published by
Princeton Architectural Press
37 East Seventh Street
New York, NY 10003

For a catalog of books published by Princeton Architectural Press, call toll free 800.722.6657
or visit www.papress.com

Editor & book design: Mark Lamster
Jacket design: Sara E. Stemen
Drawings & Plans: Dan Herman & Linda Chung

Acknowledgments: I would like to thank my colleagues at Esto Photographics, especially
Kent Draper and Laura Bolli; Mary Doyle and Mike Kimines of TSI for their help in
preparing these images; and Mark Lamster for his support from start to finish—Erica Stoller

Princeton Architectural Press acknowledges Ann Alter, Eugenia Bell, Jan Cigliano, Jane
Garvie, Caroline Green, Beth Harrison, Clare Jacobson, Mirjana Javornik, Therese Kelly,
Leslie Ann Kent, Sara Moss, Anne Nitschke, Lottchen Shivers, and Jennifer Thompson of
Princeton Architectural Press—Kevin C. Lippert, publisher

For the licensing of Ezra Stoller images, contact Esto Photographics.
Fine art reproductions of Stoller prints are available through the James Danziger Gallery.

Printed in Hong Kong.

Library of Congress Cataloging-in-Publication Data
Frank Lloyd Wright's Fallingwater / photographs by Ezra Stoller ;
  introduction by Neil Levine.
      p.   cm. -- (Building Blocks)
  Includes bibliographical references.
  ISBN 1-56898-203-8 (cloth : alk. paper)
  1. Wright, Frank Lloyd, 1867–1959, Contributions in domestic
  architecture. 2. Fallingwater (Pa.) Pictorial works. 3. Kaufmann family--
  Homes and Haunts Pictorial works. I. Stoller, Ezra. II. Title: Fallingwater.
  III. Series: Building blocks series (New York, N.Y.)
  NA737.W7A4   1999c
  782'.372'092--dc21   99-35129
                                                         CIP